TH̲ ̲ ̲ ̲ ̲URS

in the Western United States

©1993 Dinamation International Corp.   ALLOSAURUS

by **William D. Panczner**

Cover illustration of *Deinonychus* and several interior illustrations by Jon T. Gunderson

A RENAISSANCE HOUSE PUBLICATION

ISBN: 1-55838-149-X

RENAISSANCE HOUSE

A Division of Jende-Hagan, Inc.
541 Oak Street ~ P.O. Box 177
Frederick, CO 80530

10 9 8 7 6 5 4 3 2 1

CONTENTS

Some of the photographs in this book were provided by Dinamation International Corp., a manufacturer of robotically-animated traveling exhibitions for museums, zoos and aquariums worldwide. This interactive exhibitry allows children and adults to experience dinosaurs, mammals, whales and sea creatures in a non-threatening environment. For information on Dinamation's exhibition locations, call 1-800-547-0503.

This book is dedicated to the author's family, "who always encouraged and allowed me to bring dreams into reality." Bill Panczner, from Arlington, Texas, is a geologist, science educator, photographer, writer, museum designer and former curator. Jon Gunderson, from Dallas, Texas, is a commercial design artist and illustrator. Special thanks goes to the author's daughter and son, Shawna and Chris; to Drs. Wann Langston and Edwin Colbert for their comments on the text pertaining to TX, OK, NM & AZ. And to Ken Carpenter, Peter Dodson, Robert Raynolds, and Dan Grenard for their critical reviews and comments.

WELCOME

Our knowledge of dinosaurs comes principally from their fossilized remains. According to Peter Dodson of the Dinosaur Society--a group of scientists, writers, artists, and aficionados--scientists have uncovered only about 2,100 complete dinosaur skeletons. It is extremely rare to find a complete skeleton; most specimens must be assembled from bits and pieces of skeletal remains.

For fossils to form, a creature must be buried by sediments very soon after its death. The quicker it is covered, the better the chances that an intact fossil will be formed. Soft body parts usually decompose, leaving only hard skeletal structures to fossilize. In rare instances, soft parts of an organism do fossilize, making a most important record. The processes of fossilization and lithification (turning to rock) occur simultaneously. Through the dynamic geologic forces of folding, faulting, uplifting, and erosion, the remains are slowly exposed on the earth's surface once again.

Other remains, such as tracks, nests, eggs, and dung (coprolites), have yielded some of our newer dinosaur knowledge. Thanks to the latest medical and scientific laboratory equipment, and the addition of many different scientific disciplines, scientists are now beginning to learn about dinosaurs' lifestyles, behavior, types of diet, appearance, and the environmental conditions in which they lived.

This book is organized chronologically by geologic periods. The dinosaurs were selected for their uniqueness, as well as to give a good cross-section of the hundreds of species that roamed the western U.S. The locations noted are where dinosaur remains have most often been found. Data was compiled from sources current to 1993, but because the study of dinosaurs is evolving, and new theories being offered, our understanding of these remarkable creatures is continually changing.

At field locations suggested, travelers can see where dinosaurs roamed and where remains have been found. However, there are not necessarily remains in these locations today. _Please_, _remember:_ dinosaur remains are a valuable scientific resource. DO NOT remove fossils, rocks, plants, or animals from federal, state, or Indian lands. ALWAYS get permission to enter private property. NEVER disturb or remove any remains from the ground or rock strata; report their location to an educational institution. It is important not only to respect and protect fossils, but to preserve the environment of living plants and animals and the delicate ecosystems in which they exist. Stewardship and preservation of our natural areas are essential.

THE FIRST TWO STAGES OF FOSSIL FORMATION

THE GEOLOGIC PAST

Scientists now believe that the earth formed out of the vast void of the cosmos about 4.6 billion years ago. Slowly the surface cooled, and by 4 billion years ago the earth's crust had stabilized. An atmosphere formed out of gases emitted from erupting volcanoes.

The basins of this primordial surface filled with rain water, forming the oceans. Over the next half-billion years, single-celled organisms developed within the seas. Slowly these simple life forms evolved into more complex multicellular organisms. About a billion years ago, simple worm-like creatures began to make burrows into the soft sediments of the ocean floor. Up to this point, animal life consisted of creatures made up of soft parts that left few fossils or traces.

Then, about 600 million years ago, animals with hard parts began to develop. These creatures fossilized and left records of their existence. Life in the seas diversified greatly. By 400 million years ago, animal and plant life had spread from the sea and began to develop on land. Amphibians evolved, which could live both on land and in water. Eventually these animals lost their dependence on a water environment and became primarily land dwellers: the reptiles. Land plants flourished; a new world was developing.

Early reptiles fed on insects and other animals, but some developed a taste for plant life. As their eating habits specialized, they became either plant eaters (herbivores) or meat eaters (carnivores). With the passage of time, some of these early reptiles grew more upright in their stance. Slowly they spread throughout the developing continental interior plains.

One group of reptiles were small, extremely active carnivores, found along the lakes, rivers, and borders of

Jon T. Gunderson
THE LAST TWO STAGES OF FOSSIL FORMATION

the early seas. About 245 million years ago, these lizard-like creatures began to appear--the early ancestors of the dinosaurs.

Over the last 300 million years, several events occurred that are referred to by scientists as mass extinction events. During these cataclysms, half to three-quarters of plant and animal life ended. Dinosaurs lived through two such events, and were able to adapt to their surroundings and diversify among the space left vacant by other animals. But the last great mass extinction event, occurring 65 million years ago, ended their reign. Still, nearly half the plant and animal groups then on land and sea did manage to survive. Scientists are continually studying these events to determine what caused them and why some life forms survived while others perished.

Jon T. Gunderson   TRACKWAYS: FOOT PRINTS

Jon T. Gunderson

SETTING THE STAGE

Dinosaur remains have been found on every continent, some dating back more than 225 million years. These creatures existed on earth for more than 160 million years, successfully adapting to the changes in their environment. There are approximately 300 different dinosaur species, but the number keeps increasing with research from new dig sites.

The Triassic Period: 245 to 208 Million Years Ago

At the beginning of the Triassic Period, some 245 million years ago, the earth's surface was essentially a single land mass, a supercontinent called Pangaea, that reached almost from pole to pole.

Evidence indicates that the Early Triassic Period had a cool, dry climate, but became warmer with wet summers and dry winters. Because of this weather pattern, much of the continental soil, rich in iron, began to rust or oxidize. This chemical action formed red bedrock in such places as the famous Chinle Formation in the southern Rocky Mountains.

By the Late Triassic, barren sandy desert conditions extended over much of Pangaea's interior. The mountains formed during this period weathered to low hills. Plant life, too, was evolving; some forms developed and diversified while others became extinct. Plants that were common in the warm, moist climate of the coastlines and rivers of the Triassic included ferns, horsetails, cycads, ginkgos, tree ferns, and conifers.

The ancestors of the dinosaurs that evolved at the beginning of the Triassic became an important animal life form. During this period, small, fast, meat eating animals were common, but by the Middle to Late Triassic, plant eating animals had become plentiful. As some of these plant eaters became extinct, carnivores

HIP BONE STRUCTURES

developed to take their places. During the Middle Triassic, these reptiles ruled the earth.

The earliest dinosaurs appeared during the Late Triassic Period, approximately, 228 million years ago. However, footprints of three-toed creatures thought to be dinosaurs have been found in the rocks that formed 240 million years ago. No skeletal remains of these creatures have yet been found.

Scientists classify dinosaurs using a taxonomic system based on common traits. Researchers have found that dinosaurs evolved in two directions, the difference based on arrangement and structure of the hip bones. One group's hip bones were bird-like and have been placed in the order *Ornithischia*. The other group, with hip bones that were lizard-like, were classified in the *Saurischia* order.

At the end of the Triassic Period, 208 million years ago, a significant extinction event occurred. These early ancestors of the dinosaurs died out, but the *Pterosaurs* (flying reptiles) and other reptiles survived.

The Jurassic Period: 208 to 144 Million Years Ago

At the beginning of the Jurassic Period, Pangaea was still intact as a single land mass, but by the Late Jurassic, it began to break in two. The northern land mass, named Laurasia, eventually became North America, Europe, and Asia. The other super continent, Gondwanaland, evolved into South America, Africa, India, Antarctica, and Australia. As the two continental land masses moved slowly about on the earth's surface, Laurasia began to split, opening up the Atlantic Ocean. What was to become North America moved westward, while Europe and Asia drifted east. Land bridges probably existed between the masses, which allowed dinosaurs and other animal life to migrate between them. Antarctica, India, and Australia broke away from Gondwanaland and began to drift northeast. During this period, the rocks which made up the sediments of the continent's interior developed into the sandstones, mudstones, and siltstones of the famous Morrison formation, one of the richest in the western U.S. for dinosaur fossils.

A new group of dinosaurs now began to appear. Their numbers increased and they diversified to become the most important land animal of the period, with herds migrating on a regional basis. By the Middle to Late Jurassic, 187 to 144 million years ago, these extremely large plant-eating dinosaurs had become the most important creatures on earth. Their success was guaranteed by the vast amount of plant material available for food. They moved and ate continually, the larger ones browsing at tree-top level while smaller ones ate shorter trees, bushes, and ground cover. These huge creatures, some over 100 feet long, could reach 50 feet high to find food.

Earth's plant life during the Jurassic provided not only food but shelter for smaller dinosaurs and other animals. Plants continued to diversify and mammals were slowly developing as small shrew-like creatures. They lived among the plants, eating the newly developing seeds as well as insects. Although the Jurassic climate was warmer, with increased humidity, it appears that the continent's interior was drier, the moisture being concentrated near the coastlines and rivers. Increased rainfall may have allowed the vegetation to become more universal, lush, and tropical with ferns, horsetails, cycads and conifers.

As the land changed, so did the ocean currents, altering the earth's climate. Laurasia turned warm and moist; Gondwanaland became temperate. The continents grew greener and deserts became smaller. By the late Jurassic, deserts were nearly gone and large forests had developed. The polar ice caps were yet to appear.

The Cretaceous Period: 144 to 65 Million Years Ago

This geologic period was marked by dynamic changes in the developing of the continents. Some of the earth's surface subsided beneath the oceans, while other parts were raised to great heights as mountains began to form. The land masses continued to drift apart, Antarctica and Australia moving southeast while India went northeast. Africa began to split away from South America. The North American continent, which had a much longer coastline than today, was connected with Europe at Greenland and Labrador. The large seaway that began to develop during the Middle to

Late Jurassic Period, now flooded much of the interior U.S. and cut the continent in two. Uplifting was responsible for the formation of many of the world's mountain ranges during this time. Slowly the climate became warm and humid, probably much warmer than today, with alternating wet and dry seasons. The vast, shallow continental seas that covered the middle of North America were warmed by the sun.

At the beginning of the Cretaceous, the earth had no polar ice cover; later the poles began to cool. As the shallow seas intruded on many of the continental land masses, seasonal variations were greatly reduced. By the Late Cretaceous, a more pronounced global cooling is thought to have occurred, with cooler winters and warm summers. This seasonal effect became greater as the distance from the equator increased.

In the Early Cretaceous Period, the earth's land masses--including the far western side of North America-- were covered by tropical and semitropical jungles, with trees more than 60 feet tall. But other regions in the west were still semiarid. Ferns, cycads, tropical conifers, cypress and other now-extinct plants were dominant in this period. Flowering plants (angiosperms) such as willows, oaks, and palms, began to appear and developed into the most important, successful plants of the Cretaceous. These included the ancestors of today's roses, magnolias, walnuts, and oaks.

The changes in land, sea, and climate affected developing plants and animals. Life evolved differently on each continent. By the Late Cretaceous, tropical forests appeared in parts of today's western U.S., while treeless savannahs are thought to have developed closer to the equator. New species of dinosaurs continued to appear, and reptiles reigned as the dominant animal life form.

Jon T. Gunderson   COELOPHYSIS

COELOPHYSIS (see-low-FIE-sis)
"Hollowform"

This is one of the oldest dinosaurs found in the U.S. It lived about 215 million years ago in the Late Triassic Period. Remains of this meat-eating dinosaur were discovered at the Ghost Ranch, northwest of Abiquiu, NM, and east of Holbrook, AZ, in the Petrified Forest N.P.

A small bipedal predator, the *Coelophysis* was about 10 feet long, weighed less than 50 pounds and stood about 2-1/2 feet tall. It had a sleek body with a long, thin tail and neck. The pointed snout in its large, slender head contained a mouth full of sharp teeth. Muscular rear legs and bird-like feet gave it strength, speed, and agility. Its shorter front legs had hands with 3 sharp-clawed fingers, used not only to hold its prey, but to search for food.

Coelophysis likely lived near or along water, traveling and hunting in packs. It was fast enough to overtake insects and much larger animals.

MUSEUMS: NM: Ruth Hall Museum of Paleontology, Abiquiu; New Mexico Mus. of Nat. Hist. in Albuquerque; CO: the Denver Mus. of Nat. Hist. has the only mounted skeleton on display; AZ: Museum of Northern Arizona.

FIELD LOCATIONS: The discovery site is now a National Natural Landmark. Take US 84 NW from Abiquiu, NM to the Ghost Ranch. AZ: Lacey Point viewpoint is north of I-40 in the Painted Desert of the Petrified Forest, east of Holbrook. Fragments also have been found in the Painted Desert Wilderness Area.

DILOPHOSAURUS

DILOPHOSAURUS (die-LOW-fuh-SORE-us)
"Two-crested reptile"

This predator was found in Early Jurassic rocks of northeastern Arizona in 1942. The discovery was made on the Navajo Indian Reservation near Tuba City.

Dilophosaurus is thought to have measured about 20 feet long and 6 feet tall. Its long head had a most distinctive double crest on top of the skull, which is still present in the fossilized form today. Its mouth contained sharp, blade-shaped teeth. The dinosaur's large, muscular rear legs, each 3-toed with claws, probably gave the beast both speed and agility. In a fully erect walking position, it likely reached just over 4 feet tall at the hips. Scientists believe the front legs had small, 4-fingered hands, with claws on only 3 of the fingers. The *Dilophosaurus* is estimated to have weighed more than 800 pounds.

MUSEUMS: This dinosaur is displayed at the Museum of Northern Arizona, the Nat. Hist. Mus. of Los Angeles County, and the Paleontological Museum of the University of California at Berkeley. The Arizona specimen is the only articulated skeletal display of this dinosaur.

FIELD LOCATIONS: The discovery site for this efficient hunter is just west of Tuba City, AZ, about 200 yards off the "old highway" to Moenave. Trackways, probably of *Dilophosaurus*, have been found just west of the junction of US 160 and US 89.

David Greenall, at Mus. of Northern AZ   SCUTELLOSAURUS SKELETON

SCUTELLOSAURUS (skoo-TELL-o-SORE-us)
"Bony-plate or shield reptile"

This small dog-sized plant eater, that lived in what is now northeastern Arizona, was described and named in 1981 from the remains of two skeletal specimens found east of Cameron. Scientist believe slim-bodied *Scutellosaurus* had long, large rear legs and thin, short front legs. Possibly it walked on all fours, but more likely it walked and ran on its powerful rear legs--probably a fast, agile creature. When on all fours, this low, sleek beast probably stood just over a foot high at the hips.

Scutellosaurus was about 4 feet long and weighed about 20 pounds. It had a moderately long, strong tail that it likely used both for balance and defense. Several hundred small, quarter-sized bony plates or "scutes" fitted into the skin on its back, neck, ribs, and tail. The small skull is thought to have had powerful jaws with ridged, blade-like front teeth, and pointed teeth on the sides of the jaw which helped slice its food. Small claws are attached to each of its five-fingered hands. Because of its armor and general body form, some scientists believe this dinosaur was the ancestor of larger and later armored dinosaurs. This beast is thought to be the only armored dinosaur that could walk on two legs. Other armored species walked on all fours.

MUSEUMS: Exhibited at the Mus. of Northern Arizona, Flagstaff.

FIELD LOCATIONS: AZ: east of Cameron (north of Flagstaff on US 89) in the Painted Desert area of the Navajo Indian reservation. The site is SE of Rock Head Ridge on Ward Terrace.

ALLOSAURUS

ALLOSAURUS (AL-o-SORE-us)
"Other reptile"

A*llosaurus* was one of the most powerful and vicious bipedal carnivores of the Late Jurassic in what is today the western U.S. Until the appearance of the *Tyrannosaurus*, millions of years later in the Cretaceous Period, *Allosaurus* was one of the largest predators.

This was a common dinosaur with a wide hunting range throughout the region. Specimens have been found in the rocks of the Morrison Formation. Of particularly good quality are the ones from Moab, Cleveland, and Jensen, UT; Como Bluff, WY; Rabbit Valley, Grand Junction, Dinosaur Ridge near Morrison, and Garden Park near Cañon City, CO.

Scientists believe *Allosaurus* reached lengths of more than 40 feet, stood 15 feet tall, and weighed over 2 tons. Its rear legs were large and extremely powerful, probably adapted not only for speed, but for agility.

MUSEUMS: Displays of this important dinosaur can be seen in UT: Dinosaur Nat. Mon. Museum near Jensen; College of Eastern Utah Prehistoric Museum in Price; Utah Mus. of Nat. Hist. in Salt Lake City. CO: Denver Mus. of Nat. Hist.; Museum of Western Colorado in Grand Junction; TX: Fort Worth Museum of Science and History; Texas Tech Museum in Lubbock; Panhandle-Plains Historical Museum in Canyon; CA: Nat. Hist. Mus. of Los Angeles County; MT: Museum of the Rockies, Bozeman.

Bill Panczner   ALLOSAURUS FROM CLEVELAND-LLOYD QUARRY
Specimen at Fort Worth Museum of Science & History

The forelimbs appear to have been short but muscular; they had hands with 3 fingers and long, curved, dagger-like claws. These forelimbs likely were used to capture prey and to hold it while it was devoured. *Allosaurus* is thought to have had a massive neck and head with large, powerful jaws containing big razor-sharp teeth.

Some scientists say that in areas where large herds of plant-eating dinosaurs grazed, there were perhaps three *Allosaurus* per square mile. While this figure is nearly impossible to prove, it is known that there were fewer carnivores than herbivores. Since *Allosaurus* was a carnivore, it is logical that there would be fewer of this species in a grazing area than there would be herbivores. *Allosaurus* preyed on the browsing herbivores, waiting in ambush or simply overpowering them. They also scavenged food from smaller predators of the area.

FIELD LOCATIONS: UT: just before the bridge crossing the Colorado River north of Moab, a road turns off US 191 left (west) to the BLM's Mill Canyon Dinosaur Trail and Mill Site. South of Price, on SH 10, a road turns east to Cleveland and BLM's Cleveland-Lloyd Dinosaur Quarry. Just east of Vernal on US 40, turn left (north) at Jensen on SH 149 to Dinosaur Nat. Mon.

CO: west of Mack on I-70, take the Rabbit Valley exit north into the "Research Natural Area" and "Trail Through Time." West of Grand Junction on SH 340, at the junction of South Broadway, is the Riggs Hill Nature Trail; in Cañon City, a road leads north from US 50 to Garden Park and the old dinosaur quarries. Another site is north of Morrison at Dinosaur Ridge.

WY: just north of US 287 & US 30, approx. 46 miles NW of Laramie, is Como Bluff. Road leads N to base of Como Ridge, to dinosaur quarries and dig sites; another site near Greybull.

APATOSAURUS

APATOSAURUS (ah-PAT-o-SORE-us)
"Deceptive or Headless reptile"

This gentle giant of the Late Jurassic was a herbivore whose specimens have been found in the rocks of the Morrison Formation. It was discovered near Denver at Morrison, CO, in 1877. Other finds have been made at Como Bluff, WY; near Jensen, UT, at Dinosaur Nat. Mon.; Rabbit Valley and Fruita, CO; and Kenton, OK.

No complete skeleton of this dinosaur has ever been found. Nearly complete specimens have been located but without skulls attached, although in one case the skull was found just inches from the neck and is thought to have belonged to that skeleton.

These creatures are said to have grown up to 70 feet long. Probably they had small, blunt-nosed heads with small jaws containing rod-like teeth in front. Their bodies likely were attached to massive 20-foot-long necks.

Apatosaurus stood approximately 12 feet tall at the shoulders, 15 feet tall at the hips and had a 30-foot-long tail that weighed several tons and ended in a slender whip. The belly of its heavy, bulging mid-section hung little more than 3 feet off the ground. Solid, column-shaped legs supported its 30 or more tons.

Apatosaurus had a single claw on the inside of each front foot. Even though it walked and stood on all fours, it is thought that it could lift its front feet off the ground and perhaps stand on its hind legs to browse at tree-top levels of 35 feet or more. This dinosaur probably was larger than an 18-wheeler tractor-trailer truck of today!

Apatosaurus constantly moved in search of food and browsed continually. These animals ripped conifers, but because they had no masticating (chewing) teeth they swallowed small stones (gastroliths) to grind the food in their gizzards. In one large skeletal specimen, more than 60 gastroliths were recovered. *Apatosaurus* may have traveled in herds, with adults moving on the outside and younger members of the herd on the inside, although most skeletal finds are of solitary individuals.

Apatosaurus represents one of the best examples of how scientific understanding of dinosaurs has changed. In 1877, scientist Othniel C. Marsh's field crew uncovered an immature dinosaur skeleton at Morrison, CO, which he named *Apatosaurus*. In 1879 he discovered a larger skeleton at Como Bluff, WY, and named it *Brontosaurus*. After careful study, it was found that the *Brontosaurus* was really a mature *Apatosaurus*, and so the name *Brontosaurus* was discredited.

It was long thought that because of its great size and weight, *Apatosaurus* must have lived in a shallow, swampy, water environment. This, too, was incorrect. In studying the footprints left by this creature, scientists found that it lived in semi-dry environments although it may have frequented marshy areas in search of food. There was also a theory that *Apatosaurs* dragged their tails on the ground, but in studying the trackways of these creatures, scientists found no fossil evidence of tail marks. Nor was there evidence of any damage to the tail bones from such dragging. Recent studies have shown the tails to be extremely muscular. They were carried off the ground and their swaying motion helped to keep the creatures balanced when walking. Fossil trackways also proved that *Apatosaurus* did not waddle, as was first thought, but toed a straight line, like many animals of today.

FIELD LOCATIONS: WY: Como Bluff, sites are just north of the highway in the low hills. UT: Travelers can see bones but not complete skeletons near Jensen at Dinosaur Nat. Mon. CO: near Mack at Rabbit Valley, and at Fruita, (turn south off I-70 on SH 340 to Dinosaur Hill Nature Trail); west of Denver in Morrison, take Alameda Ave. (SH 26) west from Denver. Just after crossing C-470, the road loops around Dinosaur Ridge. OK: Cimarron River Valley in northwestern OK has dig sites at 6 quarries, located 8 miles east of Kenton, just off of SH 64.

MUSEUMS: Dinosaur Nat. Mon. Museum near Jensen, UT; the Geological Museum at Laramie, WY; and the Oklahoma Mus. of Nat. Hist. at Norman.

David Peters BRACHIOSAURUS

BRACHIOSAURUS (BRACK-e-o-SORE-us)
"Arm reptile"

Called "giraffe Dinosaur" because of its body shape and nearly 30-foot-long neck, this creature of the Late Jurassic has been found both in the western U.S. and Africa, in what were once semiarid plains. *Brachiosaurus* was discovered in 1900 near Grand Junction, CO, at Riggs Hill. Other specimens have been found in rocks of the Morrison Formation at Fruita, CO, and at Garden Park, north of Cañon City.

What is known of this dinosaur was learned by studying a nearly complete skeletal specimen on display in Berlin. Recently another skeleton went on display in Chicago, modeled primarily after the Berlin specimen. *Brachiosaurus* probably stretched up to 80 feet or more--longer than two large school buses--and weighed as much as 80 tons. This is one of the largest known dinosaurs of the period.

This herbivore had an unusual body shape compared to other 4-legged dinosaurs. Scientists say its slender front legs were much longer than its stout rear legs. Thus the front of the body was high off the ground, so high that the smaller plant-eating dinosaurs could walk underneath it. The beast stood over 18 feet tall at the top of the shoulders! In its giraffe-like stance, it likely could reach more than 40 feet to browse on the upper branches of conifer trees. Its relatively short tail was used for balance when it reached into high branches.

Brachiosaurus's skull seems small in comparison to

17

its overall body size, with large, snorkel-like nostrils between and just in front of its eyes. The brain was similar in size to that of a modern-day house cat. The jaw was weak and the mouth contained rod-like teeth in front. Like other large plant-eaters, *Brachiosaurus* had to swallow small stones to grind the food in its gizzard. *Brachiosaurus* and its other large 4-legged, plant-eating brethren traveled in herds in search of food and ate continually. Because of their great size, they had few natural enemies.

MUSEUMS: No specimens of *Brachiosaurus* are currently on display in the western U.S. A skull will be displayed at the Denver Mus. of Nat. Hist. in late 1995.

FIELD LOCATIONS: CO: west of Grand Junction at Riggs Hill, and at Garden Park, north of Cañon City.

DIPLODOCUS (duh-PLOD-o-kus)
"Double beam"

Diplodocus was a common dinosaur, thought to be extremely social, for it traveled in herds in its constant search for food. A relative of *Apatosaurus*, it lived in semi-arid environments with other large herbivores and inhabited the western U.S. during the late Jurassic. Specimens have been found near Greybull, Como Bluff, and Freezeout Hills, WY, and near Jensen, UT at Dinosaur Nat. Mon. Colorado locations include Rabbit Valley, south of Fruita; Garden Park, north of Cañon City; and Dinosaur Ridge, north of Morrison.

Diplodocus had a long, slender, flexible neck and a small, narrow skull with a spoon-shaped snout. Its brain was about the size of a modern house cat's. The jaw was small and weak, with long, slender rod-like teeth in the front, designed for browsing. Like its relatives, it swallowed small stones to grind its food. *Diplodocus*'s tail was much longer then *Apatosaurus's* and apparently was used both for balance and defense.

This animal weighed little more than 20 tons and so was much quicker than its heavier relatives. It may have reached speeds of up to 15 m.p.h. in short spurts. Like *Apatosaurus*, *Diplodocus* was longer than an 18-wheel tractor-trailer, reaching lengths of 90 feet.

MUSEUMS: *Diplodocus* specimens and exhibits can be seen at the Denver (CO) Mus. of Nat. Hist., the Utah Field House of Nat. Hist. S.P. at Vernal; Dinosaur Nat. Mon. Mus. near Jensen, UT; and the Houston (TX) Mus. of Nat. Hist.

FIELD LOCATIONS: UT: Dinosaur Nat. Mon.; CO: Rabbit Valley, south of Fruita at Dinosaur Hill; Garden Park north of Cañon City; and at Morrison; WY: Como Bluff and Freezeout Hills; Greybull, in the Bighorn River Basin along US 16 and US 20.

← ← ←   Denver Mus. of Nat. Hist.   DIPLODOCUS
         (Story p.18)

STEGOSAURUS (STEG-o-SORE-us)
"Plated" or "Roofed reptile"

The state fossil of Colorado is one of the better-known dinosaurs because of its uniquely shaped armor and spiked tail. There were two species of *Stegosaurus*, which varied by size and in number of spikes on the tail. This herbivore of the western U.S. was relatively common in the Late Jurassic period. Several outstanding specimens have been found in the sediments west of Alcova and Como Bluff, WY. In Colorado, fossils have been taken from Dinosaur Ridge north of Morrison, and north of Cañon City at Garden Park. Other discovery sites are near the towns of Jensen, Price, and Moab, UT, and Kenton, OK.

The vegetation of the forest and bushlands probably offered *Stegosaurus* not only protection but an excellent source of food. Its head was small, with a long, pointed snout that was close to the ground; it preferred ground cover plants for food. Its jaw was weak, with leaf-shaped teeth, and it used its beak to rip the vegetation.

Scientists say *Stegosaurus* walked on all fours. Its forelegs were shorter than the rear, and its feet were stumpy, with 4 short toes on the front and 3 on the rear feet. It was tallest at the hips--up to 10 feet--and stretched 24 feet long, about the size of a military tank.

Stegosaurus's unique feature was two rows of large triangular bony plates, some up to 3 feet tall, that extended from its head along the back and ended with a cluster of spikes at the tip of its tail. These plates were at first thought to be protective, but recent studies

19

STEGOSAURUS

indicate that they were very porous, enabling blood to flow through them to be cooled. Although there is no evidence, some scientists think these "radiator plates" moved from side to side, allowing the breeze to cool the bulky beast. They may also have been for display to attract a mate, or for threatening other dinosaurs.

With all these bony plates and its 2-ton weight, *Stegosaurus* was slow and less agile than other dinosaurs. It was thought that the small skull contained a brain of like size. It was also believed that the animal had a large nerve center in the hip area of the spine to assist in control of its back legs, but contemporary scientists are questioning this.

MUSEUMS: CO: Denver Mus. of Nat. Hist. (one skeleton mounted; one still in the rock); Morrison Mus. of Nat. Hist. (bones still in the rock); Museum of Western Colorado in Grand Junction. UT: Utah Mus. of Nat. Hist. at Salt Lake City; Dinosaur Nat. Mon. Mus. near Jensen; College of Eastern Utah Prehistoric Museum in Price. CA: Nat. Hist. Mus. of Los Angeles Co. in Los Angeles. A replica of a "baby" or juvenile found at Dinosaur Nat. Mon. is on display in the museum there. Scattered on the cliff face of the quarry are the bones of more juvenile *Stegosaurus*.

FIELD LOCATIONS: *Stegosaurus* remains may be present at some of the same sites where *Allosaurus* and *Apatosaurus* fossils have been located. WY: Como Bluff; just west of Alcova, SW of Casper on SH 220. CO: Dinosaur Ridge north of Morrison; Grand Junction; Cañon City. UT: near Price and Moab. OK: Kenton.

Bill Panczner   LIFE-SIZE ACROCANTHOSAURUS MODEL
at Ft. Worth Museum of Science & History

ACROCANTHOSAURUS

(AK-ro-KAN-thuh-SORE-us)   *"Top spined reptile"*

This active predator was big for a carnivore, averaging 30 feet long. What scientists know about it comes from a few, incomplete specimens, but tracks are plentiful, especially in north central Texas near Glen Rose. It was discovered in Oklahoma near Atoka, but specimens also have been found near Idabel.

Acrocanthosaurus probably had a large head, but there is no evidence of a crest on the two known skulls. Its jaw was strong and its mouth filled with knife-shaped teeth. Studies show this dinosaur had small forelegs and muscular rear legs, with a moderately long, narrow tail. At the hips, it stood about 10 feet tall. *Acrocanthosaurus* weighed up to 3 tons, but was fast and agile. Scientists have estimated it walked faster than 3 m.p.h. and could exceed speeds of 20 m.p.h., despite being slightly pigeon-toed.

An interesting feature of this dinosaur was the long, 18-inch-tall sail that ran down the back of its spine, from the neck to the base of the tail. It is thought that the sail controlled the creature's body heat while it was in pursuit of its prey. Such a feature would have allowed *Acrocanthosaurus* to continue hunting when others stopped from heat exhaustion.

MUSEUMS: Oklahoma Mus. of Nat. Hist. in Norman, and the Fort Worth (TX) Mus. of Science and History.

FIELD LOCATIONS: TX: At Glen Rose is Dinosaur Valley S.P., 4 miles north of US 67 on Farm Road 205. Along the Paluxy River are numerous trackways. Near Millsap, in SW Parker Co. (Millsap is north of I-20, west of Fort Worth on Farm Road 1543.) Also near Bridgeport in Wise Co., and Bowie in Montague Co.; OK sites: west of Atoka on US 75 and south of Idabel on US 259.

FIELD LOCATION GUIDE

ARIZONA:

1 Cameron: East of Cameron in northeastern AZ; north of Flagstaff on US 89 in the Painted Desert area of the Navajo Indian Reservation; southeast of Rock Head Ridge on Ward Terrace. *Scutellosaurus.*

2 Tuba City: In northeastern AZ on the Navajo Indian Reservation, at the junction of US 160 & 89. Site is just west of Tuba City about 200 yards off the "old highway" toward Moenave. *Dilophosaurus.*

3 Lacey Point: North of I-40 in the Painted Desert portion of Petrified Forest National Park, east of Holbrook. Go north, into the Painted Desert Wilderness Area. *Coelophysis.*

COLORADO:

4 Rabbit Valley: West of Mack on I-70, take the Rabbit Valley exit north into the "Research Natural Area" and "Trail Through Time." *Allosaurus, Apatosaurus, Diplodocus.*

5 Grand Junction: West of Grand Junction, at the junction of SH 340 and South Broadway, is the Riggs Hill Dinosaur Nature Trail. *Allosaurus, Brachiosaurus, Stegosaurus.*

6 Fruita: Turn south off I-70 on SH 340 to the Dinosaur Hill Nature Trail. *Apatosaurus, Diplodocus.*

7 Garden Park: From Cañon City, a road leads north from US 50 to Garden Park and the old dinosaur quarries. *Allosaurus, Brachiosaurus, Diplodocus, Stegosaurus.*

8 Morrison: Located southwest of Denver. Take Alameda Ave. (SH 26) west from Denver. Just after crossing C-470, the trail loops around Dinosaur Ridge. *Apatosaurus, Diplodocus, Stegosaurus, Allosaurus.*

9 Littleton: Southwest of Littleton, west of C-470. *Tyrannosaurus.*

10 Green Mountain: On the eastern side of Green Mountain, just east of C-470 and vicinity. *Struthiomimus, Triceratops.*

MONTANA:

11 Jordan: On SH 200, turn north on the Hell Creek Rec. Area road to the Hell Creek formation. *Ankylosaurus, Edmontosaurus, Triceratops, Tyrannosaurus.*

12 Cow Island: In the Missouri River, north and east of Winfred, which is 38 miles north of Lewistown on SH 236. *Struthiomimus.*

13 Judith River Basin: Northwest of Winfred on SH 236. *Struthiomimus.*

14 Choteau: Northwest of Great Falls on US 89. Site is west of Choteau, under ownership of the Nature Conservancy. *Maiasaura.*

15 Fort Peck Lake: Go east of Jordan on SH 200 to SH 24, then north to Fort Peck Lake. Sites are in the hills above the lake on the eastern shore, west of Weldon. *Tyrannosaurus.*

16 Southwest of Livingston: *Apatosaurus,* maybe *Diplodocus.*

17 Makoshika State Park: Southeast of Glendive, just off I-94. *Triceratops.*

18 Warren: Yale Quarry, in the Bighorn Wilderness Area of southern MT and northern WY. Go northeast of Warren on US 310. (Warren is 65 miles south of Billings.) *Tenontosaurus, Deinonychus.*

19 Middle Dome: Near Harlowton. *Tenontosaurus.*

NEW MEXICO:

20 Ghost Ranch: Take US 84 northwest from Abiquiu. Site is now a National Natural Landmark. *Coelophysis.*

21 Seneca: North of Clayton on SH 370 near Clayton Lake S.P. *Apatosaurus, Allosaurus.*

OKLAHOMA:

22 Kenton: In the Cimarron River Valley of extreme northwestern OK. Dig sites, consisting of six quarries, are 8 miles east of Kenton, just off SH 64. *Apatosaurus, Stegosaurus, Allosaurus.*

23 Atoka: West of the town, on US 75. *Acrocanthosaurus, Tenontosaurus.*

24 Idabel: South of the town, on US 259. *Acrocanthosaurus.*

25 Lehigh: South of the town, on US 75. *Tenontosaurus.*

SOUTH DAKOTA:

26 Faith: North and east of town, off US 212. *Edmontosaurus, Tyrannosaurus, Triceratops.*

27 Buffalo: Near the town on US 85. *Triceratops, Tyrannosaurus, Iguanodon.*

TEXAS:

28 Nocona: North of the town on Farm Road 137, near Spanish Fort, along the Red River. *Iguanodon.*

29 Marathon: North of the town, west of US 385 on the western slopes of the Glass Mountains. *Iguanodon.*

30 Big Bend National Park: South of Marathon on US 385 at Tornillo Flat. *Edmontosaurus, Tyrannosaurus.*

31 Bowie: In Montague County on US 81. *Acrocanthosaurus.*

32 Bridgeport: In Wise County on SH 114. *Acrocanthosaurus.*

33 Millsap: West of Fort Worth in southwestern Parker Co., north of I-20 on Farm Road 1543. *Acrocanthosaurus, Tenontosaurus.*

34 Glen Rose: 4 miles north of US 67 on Farm Road 205, Dinosaur Valley S.P. is along the Paluxy River. *Acrocanthosaurus.*

UTAH:

35 Moab: 15 mi. north of the bridge crossing the Colorado River north of Moab, a road turns off US 191 left (west) to the BLM's Mill Canyon Nature Trail and Mill Site. Brochure available for self-guided tour. *Allosaurus, Stegosaurus, Deinonychus.*

36 Price: South of Price on SR 10, a road turns east to Cleveland and the BLM's Cleveland-Lloyd Dinosaur Quarry. Mounted specimens and *in-situ* displays; world's largest source of *Allosaurus* bones. *Allosaurus, Stegosaurus.*

37 Jensen: Just east of Vernal on US 40, turn left (north) at Jensen on SH 149 to Dinosaur Nat. Mon. *Allosaurus, Apatosaurus, Diplodocus, Stegosaurus.*

38 Dalton Well: 20 miles north of Moab on US 191. Site is about 200 yards east of the highway on state land. *Iguanodon.*

WYOMING:

39 Lovell: 22 miles north of Warren, MT, on US 310, along Crooked Creek. *Deinonychus, Tenontosaurus.*

40 Como Bluff: Just north of US 287 & US 30, approximately 30 miles northwest of Laramie. A road leads north to the base of Como Ridge and the famous dinosaur quarries and dig sites. *Allosaurus, Apatosaurus, Diplodocus, Stegosaurus.*

41 Lance Creek: North of Lusk on SH 270, near the creek. *Edmontosaurus, Triceratops, Tyrannosaurus.*

42 Alcova: Site is just west of Alcova, which is southwest of Casper on SH 220. *Stegosaurus.*

43 Greybull: In the Bighorn River Basin along US 16 and US 20. *Diplodocus, Allosaurus.*

> NOTE: These locations are sites where fossils, skeletal remains, or other indications of dinosaur life have at one time been found. Not all of them are "active" sites today. Please refer to the numbers on pgs. 24 & 25.

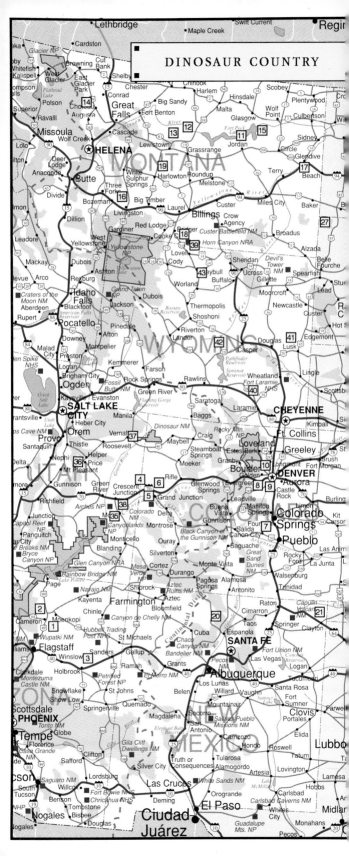

DINOSAUR COUNTRY

ARIZONA

1. *Scutellosaurus*
2. *Dilophosaurus*
3. *Coelophysis*

COLORADO

4. *Allosaurus, Apatosaurus, Diplodocus*
5. *Allosaurus, Brachiosaurus Stegosaurus*
6. *Apatosaurus, Diplodocus*
7. *Allosaurus, Brachiosaurus, Diplodocus, Stegosaurus*
8. *Apatosaurus, Diplodocus, Stegosaurus, Allosaurus*
9. *Tyrannosaurus*
10. *Struthiomimus, Triceratops*

MONTANA

11. *Ankylosaurus, Edmontosaurus, Triceratops, Tyrannosaurus*
12. *Struthiomimus*
13. *Struthiomimus*
14. *Maiasaura*
15. *Tyrannosaurus*
16. *Apatosaurus, Diplodocus*
17. *Triceratops*
18. *Tenontosaurus, Deinonychus*
19. *Tenontosaurus*

NEW MEXICO

20. *Coelophysis*
21. *Apatosaurus, Allosaurus*

OKLAHOMA

22. *Apatosaurus, Stegosaurus, Allosaurus*
23. *Acrocanthosaurus, Tenontosaurus*
24. *Acrocanthosaurus*
25. *Tenontosaurus*

SOUTH DAKOTA

26. *Edmontosaurus, Tyrannosaurus, Triceratops*
27. *Triceratops, Tyrannosaurus, Iguanodon*

TEXAS

28. *Iguanodon*
29. *Iguanodon*
30. *Edmontosaurus, Tyrannosaurus*
31. *Acrocanthosaurus*
32. *Acrocanthosaurus*
33. *Acrocanthosaurus, Tenontosaurus*
34. *Acrocanthosaurus*

UTAH

35. *Allosaurus, Stegosaurus, Deinonychus*
36. *Allosaurus, Stegosaurus*
37. *Allosaurus, Apatosaurus, Diplodocus, Stegosaurus*
38. *Iguanodon*

WYOMING

39. *Deinonychus, Tenontosaurus*
40. *Allosaurus, Apatosaurus, Diplodocus, Stegosaurus*
41. *Edmontosaurus, Triceratops, Tyrannosaurus*
42. *Stegosaurus*
43. *Diplodocus, Allosaurus*

NOTE: For additional information regarding the locations of these sites, please refer to the Field Location Guide on pages 22 and 23 of this publication.

© 1993 Dinamation International Corp.

DEINONYCHUS

DEINONYCHUS (die-NON-ick-us)
"Terrible claw"

This small, carnivorous animal, more closely related to birds than other dinosaurs, was discovered in 1964 in Montana, south of Billings near Warren at the Yale Quarry in the Big Horn River basin. Remains have also been found at Crooked Creek near Lovell, WY.

Even though *Deinonychus* was small, it was not intimidated by the size of its generally larger prey. Scientists believe the animal was less than 11 feet long, weighed about 175 pounds and stood approximately 3 feet tall at the hips. It had a large brain and a well-developed nervous system. *Deinonychus's* large head contained knife-sharp teeth and extremely muscular jaws. These features, along with large eyes for keen eyesight, a strong flexible neck, large claws on both its hands and feet, and its speed made it a highly specialized, dangerous predator. It was quite agile, and probably could jump and leap.

Its skeletal bones, even though light weight, seem to have been extremely strong. Evidence indicates that *Deinonychus* had long forearms, and hands consisting of three independently moving fingers with large claws, which allowed it to capture and hold its prey. It had strong muscular rear legs with feet that were quite unique. Many bipedal predators had feet with 3 thin toes that pointed forward and a smaller toe pointing backwards (although this is rare in footprints). But tracks show that *Deinonychus's* feet had a more bird-like configuration. Its first toe was very short; the second was long with a large 7-inch sickle-shaped claw

Jon T. Gunderson   THE CRETACEOUS WORLD

attached. The third and fourth toes were long, but without the large sickle-shaped claw. They pointed forward and had sharp claws. A strong calf muscle probably provided the power needed to control and operate the large claw. Apparently this claw was not used in walking, but could be lowered to rip open its victims.

Deinonychus's tail was long, slender, and stiff which helped to keep it balanced. The unusual bone structure of the tail likely gave this creature great maneuverability. Bony stiffening rods ran along the vertebrae in the tail, and the joint action at the point where it joined the body allowed the tail to move from side to side. Thus these dinosaurs probably could change direction in a split second while maintaining perfect balance.

Deinonychus hunted in packs. It seems to have had a social structure and tactics for hunting that allowed it to attack, kill, and devour dinosaurs larger and much heavier than itself.

MUSEUMS: Museum of the Rockies in Bozeman, MT; California Academy of Science in San Francisco.

FIELD LOCATIONS: Badlands of the Bighorn Wilderness in southern MT and northern WY. Specific areas are near Warren, 65 miles south of Billings, MT, on US 310; continue 22 miles south on the same road to Crooked Creek near Lovell, WY. Also at Middledome near Harlowton, MT.

David Peters   IGUANODON, WITH BARYONYX IN FOREGROUND

IGUANODON (ih-GWAN-o-DON)
"Iguana-tooth"

Although few remains of this dinosaur have been found in the western U.S., *Iguanodon* was one of the first dinosaurs to be scientifically described. A plant eater, it seems to have traveled both in small groups and large herds along the swampy shoreline of the regional lakes. Its horse-shaped head and blunt snout had no teeth in front, but it did have a horny beak for grasping leaves and branches. Apparently *Iguanodon* used its broad rear teeth and large cheek pouches for masticating food. Probably it lived in marshes or near other bodies of water where it feasted on ferns, horsetails, cycads, and conifers. It apparently had a long tongue, for pulling leaves and branches off trees and bushes.

This beast stretched 30 feet and weighed up to 6 tons. When it was young, its short, weak forelegs probably were not used for walking. But toward adulthood, the forelegs grew longer and stronger, an aid to walking as well as searching and grasping food. On its powerful rear legs, it could reach more than 15 feet to feed on the upper vegetation.

Iguanodon apparently had special hands with unusual fingers. The large thumb was spike-like, and the fifth finger was flexible for grasping objects. Its rear legs had feet with a 3-hooved toe configuration. A long, ridged tail extended from its back.

FIELD LOCATIONS: UT: near Moab; also Dalton Well, 20 miles N of Moab on US 191, 200 yards E of the hwy. TX: N of Nocona on Farm Road 137 near Spanish Fort, along the Red River; N of Marathon, W of US 385 on western slopes of the Glass Mts. SD: near Buffalo. Exhibited at the S.D. School of Mines.

Bill Panczner

TENONTOSAURUS SKULL
Dallas Museum of Natural History

TENONTOSAURUS (te-NON-tuh-SORE-us)
"Sinew reptile"

This dinosaur was a herbivore that preferred warm, rainy climates with cycads, ferns, and conifers to graze upon. It's believed that *Tenontosaurus* was about 20 feet long, and had a 12-foot-long stiff, heavy tail. It walked mostly on its powerful, larger rear legs with 4-toed feet. Its forelegs were strong, with feet that could be used like hands, as well as for walking or holding its food. *Tenontosaurus* had a moderately long head and long, flexible neck. It had no front teeth, but a horny beak for grasping and ripping plant material. Its rear teeth were flat, for grinding its food. From the many tracks this dinosaur left throughout the west, scientists think it lived and traveled in family groups.

Tenontosaurus roamed from Montana, where its remains were discovered in 1903, south to Wyoming and Texas. Specimens have been found near Warren and Harlowton, MT; near Lovell, WY; near Millsap, TX; and near Atoka and Lehigh, OK.

MUSEUMS: Travelers can see specimens and exhibits of *Tenontosaurus* at the Dallas (TX) Mus. of Nat. Hist. and the Fort Worth Mus. of Science & History.

FIELD LOCATIONS: Lovell, WY; near Millsap, TX; and near Atoka, OK. In MT: north and east of Warren on US 310, in an area of badlands; also Middle Dome near Harlowton. OK: the region south of Lehigh on US 75.

Jon T. Gunderson

ANKYLOSAURUS

ANKYLOSAURUS (an-KYLE-uh-SORE-us)
"Fused reptile"

This armored dinosaur lived in the Late Cretaceous Period in the Rocky Mountain region. Like most herbivores, the *Ankylosaurus* walked on 4 sturdy legs. What is known of this creature was gleaned from only three partially described specimens. The hornless beast probably reached lengths of up to 23 feet, was 6 feet wide, about 5 feet at its tallest point, and weighed nearly 4 tons--another tank-sized species.

Ankylosaurus had armor plates, but little is known about how they were arranged. The bony plates protected its nearly 3-foot-long skull, and large keeled plates (up to 12 in.) covered its body. Its only horns were on the skull, just behind the eyes. A large bony club at the end of its tail provided protection and gave it the appearance of a modern-day horny toad.

In Montana, specimens of *Ankylosaurus* have been found north of Jordan. There are no specimens on public view in the western U.S.

MUSEUMS: There is a tail club of *Euoplocephalus*, a type of ankylosaur, at the Denver Mus. of Nat. Hist.

FIELD LOCATIONS in MT: north of Jordan, in the Hell Creek formation. Jordan is on SH 200, turn north on road to the Hell Creek Rec. Area.

Jon T. Gunderson   EDMONTOSAURUS

EDMONTOSAURUS (ed-MON-tuh-SORE-us)
"Reptile from Edmonton"

Edmontosaurs were thought to be highly social animals that lived and traveled in large herds. Scientists studying the skulls of these rather common dinosaurs think they communicated with fellow members of the herd by snorts and bellows. They probably did this by means of an inflatable pouch of skin which enabled them to make deep frog-like noises.

Edmontosaurs were one of the larger types of duck-billed dinosaurs. They reached lengths of about 30 feet and weighed more than 4 tons; in a few cases they got as large as 10 tons! These beasts lived in the back regions of cypress swamps and peat bogs, in forested flood plains and bayou mud flats of the coastal plains, feeding upon the plants of these areas. This herbivore had a broad snout with large hollow nostrils, and a beak that allowed it to bite off not only leaves but branches of one of its favorite plants--conifers. Located behind the beak were grinding teeth. As these wore out, new teeth emerged to replace them in what is known as a "dental battery." The animal's lower jaw could move up and down as well as side to side, allowing it to chew its food. Thus edmontosaurs became successful plant eaters.

Edmontosaurus had large, strong hind legs for walking, and smaller front legs. Its flexible neck made it

Bill Panczner   AUTHOR (R) ON TRACKING EXPEDITION

possible for the animal to browse on ground cover up to 20 feet high. Edmontosaurs, along with the tyrannosaurs and triceratops, were among the last dinosaurs on earth before the last mass extinction event that ended their 165-million-year reign.

Edmontosaurus specimens have been found in the Laramie formation of northeastern Colorado; north of Jordan and Lewistown MT; at Lance Creek, WY; in Faith, SD; and at Tornillo Flat in Big Bend N.P., TX. The discovery of "mummies" north of Lusk at Lance Creek, WY, in 1908 gave paleontologists a chance to see excellent impressions of the skin from the head, shoulders, forearms, rear legs, and tail. So detailed were the "mummies" that even the pattern of bumps on their skin was revealed--then and now a most remarkable find.

MUSEUMS: Nat. Hist. Mus. of Los Angeles County, and the Denver Mus. of Nat. Hist.

FIELD LOCATIONS in MT: north of Jordan and Lewistown; WY: north of Lusk, near Lance Creek on SH 270; SD: north and east of Faith on US 212; TX: go south of Marathon on US 385 in Big Bend N.P. to Tornillo Flat.

Jon T. Gunderson   MAIASAURA

MAIASAURA (MY-ah-SORE-a)
"Good mother reptile"

Although this is a newly discovered species, much is known about it that has changed scientists' thinking on dinosaurs and their social behaviors. This large, plant-eating beast, discovered in 1978, was named and described the following year. Remains were found in Montana in the Two Medicine Formation west of Choteau.

Maiasaura was approximately 24 feet long and weighed about 2 tons, but specimens have been found up to 30 feet and almost double that weight. This herbivore had large, muscular rear legs and smaller forelegs, which could be used for walking, for gathering food, or tending its young. It preferred to walk on its rear legs.

The broad, flat skull of *Maiasaura* had a beak that looked like a duck's bill. The jaw was strong with no teeth in the front of its mouth, but hundreds of flattened teeth at the rear for chewing. It had large eyes, and in the middle of the forehead was a small spine. The stiff tail was used for balance when walking.

New information indicates that *Maiasaura* may have been warm-blooded. This assumption is based on its apparent rapid developmental growth. The animal lived and traveled in large breeding herds of perhaps 10,000 animals that included babies, juveniles and

33

Jon T. Gunderson   MAIASAURA EGGS IN NEST

adults. Current research indicates this dinosaur reproduced yearly.

Maiasaura nesting colonies, similar to large bird rookeries of today, contained several nests, each about 6 feet in diameter, with about 23 feet between the nests--just enough room for adults to move around without stepping on nearby nests. The female probably laid and arranged 20 to 24 lopsided, oval-shaped eggs, each about 8 inches long and weighing about a half-pound. She laid them in layers in a nest lined with plant material and covered each layer with sand. When she was done she covered the entire nest. The decomposing plant material kept the eggs warm. Parents did not sit on the nest but sat next to it to protect the eggs.

Current research indicates that new hatchlings may have been about 12 inches long and perhaps stayed in their nests approximately 60 days. By the time they left they may have reached nearly 4 feet long. It has been estimated that the newly developing young ate about 3 pounds of food daily, requiring parents to deliver to the nest between 50 and 60 pounds of food a day--mostly leaves and tender shoots of plants. To maintain themselves and their hatchlings, each parent probably had to gather about 165 pounds of plant material daily. When the plants close to the rookery were eaten, parents could have been forced to travel away from the nests for food. Probably they did this in one day and got back in time to feed their young in the evening.

Harold Malde   EGG MOUNTAIN (MT) MAIASAURA ROOKERY SITE

Maiasaura breeding herds apparently returned year after year to the same nesting site to lay their eggs and raise their hatchlings. The young increased in size annually, and by the end of the fourth year were mature adults. Other dinosaur nests, those of the small *Orodromeus*, have also been found.

Scientists studying the nests of *Maiasaura* discovered egg shells broken into small pieces, suggesting that the hatchlings stayed in the nests and crushed the shells into fragments. Skeletal remains of young dinosaurs found in the nests showed that their bones were not well-formed or developed at first, and that their teeth were worn from chewing food brought to the nests by the parents. This may indicate that the hatchlings had a powerful instinct to stay in their nests or, if they did leave, not to go far from home.

How long did these and other dinosaurs live? Some scientists think that life spans varied from species to species. But in general, the larger the mass and size, the longer the life span. A 1-ton dinosaur's life span has been estimated at about 50 years; a 5-ton's was possibly 70 years, a 25-ton specimen likely lived about 90 years, and an 80-ton dinosaur perhaps lived 120 years!

MUSEUMS: *Maiasaura* specimens are displayed at the Museum of the Rockies, Montana State Univ., in Bozeman.

FIELD LOCATIONS: West of Choteau, MT, on the Blackfoot Indian Reservation. Site is NW of Great Falls on US 89, owned by Nature Conservancy which conducts tours. North of Grand Jct., CO bones have been found that may be *Maisaura*.

Jon T. Gunderson   STRUTHIOMIMUS

STRUTHIOMIMUS (STROOTH-e-o-MY-mus)
"Ostrich mimic"

Because of its appearance, this small bird-like dinosaur has been referred to by scientists as an ostrich dinosaur. Slightly built, it stretched just over 12 feet and weighed about 200 pounds. Its small head with large eyes and bony beak was attached to the body by a slender neck. It had a long thin tail. Scientists say this animal's forelimbs were slender but strong; its hands had 3 claws attached. The long rear legs, although slender, were extremely muscular and had clawed feet.

Paleontologists believe this toothless dinosaur was primarily a plant-eater, but probably would have eaten insects and other small creatures. *Struthiomimus* was extremely fast; speeds may have reached 30 m.p.h.

Remains of *Struthiomimus* have been found at Cow Island in the Missouri River and the Judith River basin of Montana. Outside Denver, CO, near Green Mountain remains have been found of another ostrich-type dinosaur, *Ornithomimus* (a relative of *Struthiomimus*). There are presently no specimens on display of this dinosaur in the western U.S.

FIELD LOCATIONS: MT: NW of Lewistown in the Judith River basin, as well as NW of Winfred on SH 236; NE of Winfred on Cow Island in the Missouri River. CO: near Morrison on the eastern side of Green Mountain, just east of C-470.

©1993 Dinamation International Corp.   TRICERATOPS

TRICERATOPS (tri-SAIR-uh-tops)
"Three-horned face"

This abundant plant eating dinosaur of the Late Cretaceous lived in the western U.S. It favored broad forests, located in the flood plains of the western rivers, bayous and mud flats. This elephant-sized creature may have lived in herds, although it is generally found as a solitary specimen. It migrated throughout the region in search of the lush, leafy growths of ferns, cycads, and palms.

There was much variety among this family of horned dinosaurs. All had neck frills and horns on their skulls. Some had two horns over their eyes while others had three. Small neck frills were common on some, while others had large, sail-like frills. Certain species had horns or spikes on the top edges of their frills.

Triceratops had a massive, barrel-shaped body that measured up to 30 feet in length and was 10 feet tall at the hips. The legs that carried its 6-ton mass were short, the rear legs a bit longer than the front.

Perhaps its most impressive feature was its head. The largest skulls ever found were just over 7 feet long. Two large, well-developed horns grew out of the skull over the eyes. A third, smaller horn was located atop the snout, just behind the nostrils.

In front of the skull was a long beak that the animal may have used for ripping its food. The jaws were

37

Bill Panczner   DINO DIG, FORT WORTH MUS. OF SCIENCE & HISTORY

strong and muscular and contained closely packed teeth with wide grinding surfaces and cheek pouches for masticating food.

Another unique feature was the broad, bony, rounded frill at the back of the skull. This frill probably acted as a temperature control, to cool or heat the animal. It may also have served as protection or to attract a mate.

For its body and skull size, the *Triceratops's* brain was small, but it was a most successful dinosaur. One of the last to develop, it was one of the few to see the end of the reign of these great creatures.

MUSEUMS: Carter County Museum in Ekalaka, MT; the Nat. Hist. Mus. of Los Angeles County; the Kansas University Mus. of Nat. Hist. in Lawrence, KS; the Museum of Geology at the South Dakota School of Mines in Rapid City, SD; the University of Colorado Museum in Boulder, CO; the Earth Science Museum at Brigham Young University at Provo, UT; and at the Museum of the Rockies at Montana State University in Bozeman, MT.

FIELD LOCATIONS: Lance Creek and Medicine Bow, WY; Lewistown and Jordan, MT; Morrison, CO. In SD: near Buffalo on US 85; just north of Faith on US 212 in the Badlands; SW of Glendive on SH 335; and just off I-94 at Makoshika S.P. *Triceratops* remains are still being found within the city limits of Denver, CO.

©1993 Dinamation Intl. Corp.   TYRANNOSAURUS REX

TYRANNOSAURUS (tie-RAN-o-SORE-us)
"Tyrant reptile"

The most powerful and deadly carnivore of the Late Cretaceous period is probably the best-known of all dinosaurs. *Tyrannosaurus* was the largest bipedal predator ever to stalk the face of the earth. Our knowledge of "T-rex" comes from only 11 skeletal remains, found in the western U.S. and Canada, as well as Asia. Specimens were discovered in 1900 in western Montana, and in 1902 the type specimen was uncovered north of Jordan, MT. This was the specimen from which the first scientific description and work-up was done. Three years later, working from three different specimens, *Tyrannosaurus* was described.

The beast stalked its prey and waited in ambush to attack, but it also ate recently killed game. This species may have scavenged more than scientists realize, but still it was the "ultimate killing machine." Research indicates that *Tyrannosaurus* ate an average of 200 pounds of food per day, although it did not eat every day. In its estimated 60-year lifespan, it might have consumed the equivalent weight of a herd of 3,000 beef cattle--or about 400 *Triceratops*.

Tyrannosaurus was roughly 40 feet long and weighed approximately 6 tons. The largest specimen presently known is over 16 feet tall. It had a massive tail

39

Gary D. Hall   Denver Museum of Nat. History,
TYRANNOSAURUS REX

which it used for balance.

The massive rear legs were powerful, built for moderate speed and agility. It has been estimated the dinosaur's huge, clawed, 3-toed, bird-like feet could move at speeds of 3 to 5 m.p.h. or bursts up to 15 to 20 m.p.h. The beast could kick its powerful hind legs as weapons for downing its prey. Even though the front legs were small--about the size of a human arm--the 2-fingered, clawed hands could lift several hundred pounds.

Tyrannosaurus's massive (up to 4-1/2-foot-long) head held forward-looking eyes that probably gave the creature good depth of field and distance vision. Its jaws were perhaps the most powerful of all dinosaurs'. The lower jaw moved both up and down and out, helping it eat large pieces of prey quickly. *Tyrannosaurus* had 60 razor-sharp teeth, 6 to 8 inches long, varying in shape but curving backward.

MUSEUMS: Denver Mus. of Nat. Hist.; the Geological Museum, Univ. of Wyoming at Laramie; Museum of the Rockies, Montana St. Univ. at Bozeman; the Earth Science Museum, Brigham Young University at Provo, UT; the Nat. Hist. Mus. of Los Angeles County.

FIELD LOCATIONS: MT: near Jordan, take SH 200 to SH 24 north of Fort Peck. Go to the hill section above the lake on the eastern shore, west of Weldon. WY: at Lance Creek, 46 mi north of Lusk on US 85 and US 18. (This is north of Mule Creek Jct., just north of the Cheyenne River. SD: the Faith and Buffalo field sites. CO: near Littleton, west of C-470, this site is now beneath a housing development. TX: Tornillo Flat in Big Bend N.P.

J.C. Russell, USGS, BLM   MARSH QUARRY, GARDEN PARK 1884

THE GREAT BONE WARS

In the spring of 1877, two discoveries of dinosaur bones in Colorado tremendously impacted the science of paleontology. The discoveries also sparked a long and sometimes fierce feud between two renowned scientists, Edward D. Cope and Othniel C. Marsh. Their search for and description of dinosaurs has been termed "the Bone Wars" by some scientific historians.

The first discovery was on a ridge in the foothills of the Rocky Mountains near Morrison, CO. Arthur Lakes, the discoverer, sent a message and several of the bones to Othniel Marsh at Yale Univ. in New Haven, CT, asking for his assistance. When Marsh did not respond, Lakes sent a second message and bone samples to another noted scientist and fossil collector, Edward Cope of Philadelphia. Shortly, Marsh sent Lakes $100 and asked him to keep his discovery a secret, not realizing the word was already out. But by then, Cope not only knew of Lake's discovery, but was describing the bones in an article for publication! Before he could finish, however, Lakes asked Cope to send the bones to Professor Marsh at Yale, which naturally irritated Cope.

The second discovery, made by O.W. Lucas at Garden Park north of Cañon City, CO, unearthed even larger bones. Lucas sent word of his find and samples to Cope, who was very excited about this new discovery. Marsh, when he heard of the news, was extremely unhappy--not only because he had not been contacted, but because these bones were bigger, better preserved and more complete than at Morrison! He immediately dispatched his colleague and field collector, Professor Benjamin Mudge of Kansas, to check on the discovery

Bill Panczner

ALLOSAURUS ATTACKING CAMPTOSAURUS
Ft. Worth Mus. of Science & Hist.

and do some investigative digging. After some success, the work was abandoned, but Marsh's crew returned several years later and worked in the old quarries at Garden Park with outstanding results.

Next it was Marsh's turn. In the summer of 1877, he received word from W.H. Reed and W.E. Carlin of their discovery of large dinosaur bones on a bluff in Wyoming. Marsh sent a crew to explore and develop the site. By now, both he and Cope had their field crews well armed with bowie knifes, pistols and rifles to protect their sites from poaching or Indian attacks. It was said that one crew would take what it wanted from the other and destroy what was left!

Much of the Bone Wars dispute centered at the Como Bluff, WY, discovery site. Cope and his men were in the vicinity of Como Bluff in 1879 and 1880, looking for new finds. There he met Arthur Lakes who was working for Marsh. Cope's collecting crews finally moved on to Montana, and when finished at Como Bluff, Marsh and his men returned to the Denver area.

In an effort to get their finds back east for study and display as quickly and safely as possible, the men developed new field methods. One of these was to leave the partially exposed bones buried in the rock in which they were found. The rock mass containing the bones was then cut into blocks and covered with plaster or jacketed for shipping. Upon arrival, the plaster was removed and the bones extracted from the rock, studied, and mounted for display.

Marsh's and Cope's feud must not overshadow their outstanding contributions. Their work marked a turning point in the history of discovery and research on dinosaurs. Much of what is known today is the result of this rivalry in their field work. They developed field collecting methods, many of which are still in use, and made an effort to collect entire skeletal remains.

DINOSAUR EXHIBITS & PARKS

COLORADO

Garden Park Fossil Area   719-275-2331/800-876-7922
Cañon City Chamber of Commerce
PO Bin 949-Z; Cañon City, CO 81215
BLM Office, Cañon City   719-275-0631
Cañon City, CO 81215

This area was where the feud between the two great dinosaur hunters of the 1870s, E.D. Cope and O.C. Marsh began. The River Station Visitor Center recently opened. The unique Dinosaur Discovery Center will be built in the Garden Park Fossil area in the next few years. This fossil area is located north of Cañon City at Garden Park, on the road to Red Canyon Park. Guided tours are conducted during the summer.

Trail Through Time   303-241-9210
Rabbit Valley Research Natural Area

This dinosaur nature trail is located west of Mack on the north side of I-70 at the Rabbit Valley exit #2. Allow 90 minutes for this moderately strenuous 1-1/8 mi. self-guided nature loop past the Mygatt-Moore Dinosaur Quarry. Trail is managed by BLM and the Mus. of Western Colorado. Dinosaur skeletons are intact along the trail. There is periodic active dinosaur quarrying in summer months.

Picket Wire Canyonlands Dinosaur Trackway   719-384-2181
U.S. Forest Service, Comanche National Grasslands
PO Box 817 - 1321 E 3rd St.; La Junta, CO 81050

This is presently the "longest documented Dinosaur Tracksite in the world." In this 1/4-mile stretch along the Purgatoire River, more than 1,300 dinosaur tracks have been found. The site is about 30 miles south of La Junta in the U.S. Forest Service, Comanche National Grassland's Picket Wire Canyonlands. Many of these tracks may have been made by *Apatosaurus* and *Allosaurus* as they made their way along the muddy shoreline of a large shallow lake. A trail leads from CR 25, along the river about 8 miles to the site. Check at Comanche National Grasslands in La Junta for complete directions and conditions of the trail to the tracks. The U.S. Forest Service conducts 4WD trips to the tracks by reservation.

Denver Museum of Natural History   303-370-6387
2001 Colorado Blvd. (City Park)
Denver, CO 80205

In 1995, the Museum's current dinosaur exhibit will be replaced by "Prehistoric Journey," a walk through the 3.5-billion-year history of life on earth. This state-of-the-art "envirorammas" will feature dinosaurs as well as other animals and plants of each period. While construction is underway, visitors can watch dinosaurs being assembled through windows in the new gallery.

Devils Canyon Science and Learning Center   303-858-7282
Highway 340 & I-70; Fruita, CO 81521

Located near the entrance to Colorado N.M., the 22,000-sq. ft. center includes a theater, dioramas, a fossil preparation laboratory, interactive devices and displays of static and robotically-animated dinosaurs and prehistoric creatures. The center is managed by Dinamation International Society.

Because many 19th century paleontologists were from the eastern U.S., many western dinosaur skeletons are on display in museums there. Among the best eastern museums for dinosaur specimens are the Smithsonian (DC), American Mus. of Nat. Hist. (NY), Cleveland Mus. of Nat. Hist. (OH), Princeton Univ. Mus. of Nat. Hist. (NJ), Carnegie Mus. (Pittsburgh), Field Museum (Chicago), Peabody Mus. at Yale Univ. (CT), Academy of Natural Sciences of Philadelphia (Philadelphia).

National Park Service   CARNEGIE QUARRY, DINOSAUR NAT. MON.

Dinosaur Hill Nature Trail   303-241-9210
Fruita, CO 81521

This is a 45- to 60-minute, moderate 1-mile nature loop trail past a famous dinosaur quarry. It is a cooperative effort of BLM, the City of Fruita, and the Museum of Western Colorado. Nature trail is 1-1/2 miles south of Fruita on SH 340.

Dinosaur Valley   303-243-3466
362 Main Street; Grand Junction, CO 81501

Features half-size computer-controlled robotic replicas of dinosaurs, full-size skeletons, and a paleontological lab where specimens are prepared. Operated by Mus. of Western Colorado.

Dinosaur Extinction Boundary Zone

South of Trinidad, CO along I-25 near Raton Pass and the NM border is a fine exposure to the "fallout zone" between the Cretaceous-Tertiary boundary, the latter period being after the dinosaurs. This zone is made up of ash debris, rich in iridium, blown into the atmosphere when the earth was impacted by an asteroid or comet. It is thought that this event and the resulting dust generated into the atmosphere affected the flora and climate, substantially changing the dinosaurs' habitats and ending their reign.

Riggs Hill Nature Trail   303-241-9210
S. Broadway at Meadows Way
Grand Junction, CO 81501

The Riggs Hill Dinosaur Nature Trail passes Holt and Riggs Dinosaur Quarries where *Brachiosaurus* was discovered. A moderate 30- to 45- minute walk circles this 3/4-mi. loop trail. Operated by the Museum of Western Colorado. Take SH 340 west from Grand Junction to South Broadway. The trail is at the intersection of Meadows Way.

Morrison Natural History Museum   303-697-1873
Hwy. 8 (1/2) mile south of Morrison
Morrison, CO 80456

Museum contains a paleontological display as well as ecological dioramas. Jurassic dinosaur bones, originally collected by Marsh in 1877 and on loan from the Yale Peabody Museum, are being prepared here.

Dinosaur Ridge   303-697-1873
West Denver, On Alameda Pkwy., just west of C470
East of Red Rocks Park

This Ridge is held up by the Dakota Sandstone which contains over 200 dinosaur footprints as well as numerous other trace fossils. Beneath the Dakota Sandstone, the Morrison Formation is well exposed. A quarry originally worked by Marsh in 1877 is on the roadside, with dinosaur bones still exposed in the roadcut. The Friends of Dinosaur Ridge have installed a series of interpretive signs and run tours of the dinosaur remains for the public.

MONTANA

Dinosaur Extinction Boundary Zone

North of Jordan and south of Fort Peck Lake in the badlands is a large area where the iridium-rich "fallout zone" between the Cretaceous-Tertiary boundary is exposed. This boundary is world-wide but seen only where the contact zone is exposed at the earth's surface.

The Nature Conservancy   406-466-5526
Pine Butte Swamp Preserve
HC58; Box 34B; Choteau, MT 59422

In summer, the Nature Conservancy conducts the Egg Mountain Dinosaur Nesting Tour at this famous discovery site.

Museum of the Rockies   406-994-2251
Montana State University
600 W Kagy
Bozeman, MT 59324

This is the home museum for the *Maiasaura*. Excellent exhibits of other dinosaurs from Montana and the west are displayed here, including *Triceratops* and *Tyrannosaurus*. This museum also operates an outstanding summer dinosaur dig camp. (See Field Expeditions, p.48)

NEW MEXICO

Clayton Lake State Park   505-374-8808
Seneca, NM 88415

Dinosaur footprints can be seen at Clayton Lake State Park, NE of Clayton on SH 370. More than 500 footprints (including baby dinosaurs') have been found in the spillway around the dam.

OKLAHOMA

Oklahoma Museum of Natural History   405-325-4712
University of Oklahoma
1335 Asp Ave.; Norman, OK 73019

The prehistoric life displays currently at the Oklahoma Mus. of Nat. Hist. will be moved into a new and larger museum facility in the near future.

TEXAS

Dallas Museum of Natural History   214-421-DINO
Fair Park - 1st & Grand Aves.
Dallas, TX 75226

The museum is currently expanding and revamping its dinosaur exhibits. Highlights include a 32-foot-long Mosasaur, a *Tenontosaurus* and a giant prehistoric sea turtle.

Fort Worth Museum of Science & History   817-732-1631
1501 Montgomery St.; Fort Worth, TX 76107

The museum has recently renovated its dinosaur displays and built a unique dino dig area for youngsters. Major renovation and expansion of its facilities will include a prehistoric Texas gallery.

Dinosaur Valley State Park　　　　　　817-897-4588
PO Box 396; Glen Rose, TX 76043

This famous dinosaur trackway discovery site features a visitor center, life-size replicas of dinosaurs, and several miles of nature walks and trails along the Paluxy River. Be prepared to get wet.

Hondo Chamber of Commerce　　　　　210-426-3037
1600 Avenue "M"; Hondo, TX 78861

Dinosaur trackways have been found on many of the ranches in this area; several sites allow visitors for a small fee.

Heard Nat. Sci. Mus. & Wildlife Sanctuary　　214-562-5566
One Nature Place; McKinney, TX 75069

The museum has major expansion and renovation plans for its facilities and exhibits, to include prehistoric life of north Texas.

UTAH

Price River Resource Area, BLM　　　　801-637-4584
Cleveland-Lloyd Dinosaur Quarry
900 North 7th East; Price, UT 84501

This famous dinosaur quarry is a protected National Natural landmark; features a visitor center, guided tours, and a nature trail located east of Cleveland.

Dinosaur National Monument　　　　　303-374-2216
PO Box 210; Dinosaur, CO 81610

Well-known dinosaur discovery site features a visitor center and museum built around Carnegie Quarry, dinosaur displays, and a nature trail. Paleontologists no longer work the quarry face. NOTE: The museum and quarry are located in Utah; phone number and mailing address are in Colorado.

Mill Canyon Dinosaur Trail　　　　　801-259-8193
Bureau of Land Management
885 S Sand Flat Road
Moab, UT 84533

Operated by BLM, the trail is 16 miles north of Moab, 1-1/2-miles west of US 191. It is a 1/4-mile, moderately strenuous, self-guided dinosaur experience.

WYOMING

Fossil Cabin & Dinosaur Quarry　　　　307-379-2225
Medicine Bow

Fossil Cabin & Dinosaur Quarry. The original cabin, built completely of dinosaur bones, was constructed in the 1880s as a home for the dinosaur hunters working the Bone Cabin Quarry next to the cabin. It was about 15 mi. north of Como Bluff. By 1897, the original Bone Cabin was in ruins. The present cabin was built later, just off Hwy. 30, about 7 mi. east of Medicine Bow.

REFERENCES USED IN THIS BOOK

Dinosaur and Other Prehistoric Animal Factfinder, M. Benton
The Great Dinosaur Hunters and Their Discoveries, E.H. Colbert
Encyclopedia of Dinosaurs, P. Dodson
Dinosaurs, D. Dixon
The Complete T. Rex, J.R. Horner & D. Lessem
Cretaceous Airport: The Surprising Story of Real Dinosaurs, L. Jacobs
Dinosaur, D. Norman
The Illustrated Encyclopedia of Dinosaurs, D. Norman
An Odyssey in Time: The Dinosaurs of North America, D.A. Russell
Audubon Society Pocket Guides: Familiar Dinosaurs, J. Wallace
The Illustrated Encyclopedia of Pterosaurs, P. Wellnhofer
Dinosaur Digs: Places Where You Can Discover Prehistoric Creatures, R. Will & M. Read

OTHER DINOSAUR MUSEUMS

Museum of Northern Arizona
Flagstaff, AZ 86001
602-774-5211

Petrified Forest N.P.
PO Box 2217
P.F.N.P., AZ 86028
602-524-6228

— CALIFORNIA —

Museum of Paleontology
University of California
Berkeley, CA 94720
510-642-1821

**Natural History Museum
of Los Angeles County**
900 Exposition Blvd.
Los Angeles, CA 90007
213-744-3466

California Academy of Sciences
Golden Gate Park
San Francisco, CA 94118
415-221-5100

— COLORADO —

Museum of Western Colorado
248 S Fourth St.
Grand Junction, CO 81502
303-242-0971

University of Colorado Museum
Boulder, CO 80309
303-429-6165

— IDAHO —

Idaho Museum of Natural History
University of Idaho
Pocatello, ID 83209

— KANSAS —

Kansas Univ. Mus. of Nat. Hist.
Lawrence, KS 66045
913-864-4540

Sternberg Memorial Museum
Fort Hays State University
600 Park St.; Hays, KS 67601
913-628-4286

— MONTANA —

Fort Peck Museum
Fort Peck, MT 59223
406-632-5519

Carter County Museum
100 Main St.
Ekalaka, MT 59324
406-775-6886

Upper Musselshell Museum
11 S Central Ave.
Harlowtown, MT
406-632-5519

— NEBRASKA —

Univ. of NE State Mus.
14th and "U" St.
Lincoln, NE 68588
402-472-3779

— NEW MEXICO —

Ruth Hall Mus. of Paleontology
Ghost Ranch Conference Ctr.
Abiquiu, NM 87510
505-685-4333

NM Mus. of Nat. Hist.
1801 Mountain Road, NW
Albuquerque, NM 87104
505-841-8837

— SOUTH DAKOTA —

Museum of Geology
South Dakota School of Mines
Rapid City, SD 57701
605-394-2467

— TEXAS —

Brazosport Mus. of Nat. Science
400 College Drive
Brazosport, TX 77566
409-265-7831

**Corpus Christi Museum
of Science and History**
1900 N Chaparral
Corpus Christi, TX 78401
512-833-2862

Texas Memorial Museum
University of Texas
Austin, TX 78705
512-471-1604

Big Bend National Park
Big Bend N.P., TX 79834
915-477-2251

Panhandle-Plains Historical Museum
2401 Fourth Avenue
Canyon, TX 79016
806-656-2244

Houston Museum of Natural Science
1 Hermann Circle Dr.
Houston, TX 77030
713-639-4600

Museum of Texas Tech University
4th & Indiana
Lubbock, TX 79409
806-742-2442

Witte Mus. of Hist. & Sci.
3801 Broadway
San Antonio, TX 78209
210-820-2169/820-2170

— UTAH —

**College of Eastern Utah
Prehistoric Museum**
155 East Main
Price, UT 84501
801-637-5060

BYU Earth Science Mus.
Brigham Young University
1683 Canyon Rd.
Provo, UT 84602
801-378-3680

Utah Museum of Natural History
University of Utah
Salt Lake City, UT 84112
801-789-3799

**Utah Field House of
Natural History State Park**
235 East Main Street
Vernal, UT 84078
801-789-3799

Greybull Museum
325 Greybull Ave.
Greybull, WY 82426
307-765-2444

Geological Museum
University of Wyoming
Laramie, WY 82071
307-766-4218/766-3386

FIELD EXPEDITIONS

These special programs are designed to encourage dinosaur enthusiasts in field research. There are experiences for all ages, including children. Some also offer financial help or college credit for teachers.

Museum of the Rockies - Paleo Field School
Montana State University; 600 West Kagy Blvd.
Bozeman, MT 59717; 406-994-2251

A summer field program conducted at Egg Mountain near Choteau, Montana. Various programs for all ages, child to adult.

The Nature Conservancy - Pine Butte Guest Ranch
HC 58, Box 34C; Choteau, MT 59422; 406-466-2158

A non-profit conservation organization owns this rustic facility; offers natural history tours and workshops and programs for children. Includes the Egg Mountain Maiasaura nesting site.

Dinosaur Discovery Expeditions
PO Box 307; Fruita, CO 81521; 800-DIG-DINO (344-3466)

A division of Dinamation International (see below) that runs trips to assist in summer dinosaur field work. Usually in Colorado, Utah, or Wyoming, but also has sites worldwide. Sponsors camps for children (6-12).

Foundation for Field Research   619-445-9364
PO Box 2010; Alpine, CA 91903

Works with scientists who need volunteer help with paleontological projects in the U.S. and Mexico.

International Research Expeditions   415-323-4228
140 University Drive; Menlo Park, CA 94025

Works with scientists who need volunteer help in their dinosaur field projects in the Rocky Mountain region.

DINOSAUR RELATED ORGANIZATIONS

The Dinosaur Society Inc.
200 Carleton Avenue
East Islip, NY 11730
516-277-7855

Dinosaur Nature Assoc.
1291 East Hwy. 40
Vernal, UT 84078
801-789-8807

Nature Conservancy, Inc.
1815 North Lynn St.
Arlington, VA 22209

The Garden Park Paleontology Soc.
PO Box 313
Cañon City, CO 81215

Friends of the Dinosaurs
Geological Museum
University of Wyoming
Laramie, WY 82071
307-766-4218

Friends of Dinosaur Ridge
Morrison Natural History Museum
PO Box 564
Morrison, CO 80465
303-697-1873

Western Interior Paleo Society
PO Box 20011
Denver, CO 80220

Dinamation International Society
PO Box 307
Fruita, CO; 303-858-7282

A non-profit organization promoting education, research and preservation of fossil resources. The Society is open to membership and offers the world's largest participant-funded dinosaur dig program, Dinosaur Discovery Expeditions (see above).